Contents

GW00482237

HOW TO PLAY YOUR KALIMBA

- Hold the kalimba with your your thumb on the keys and your other fingers on the side.
- Using your nails to strike the keys will minimize finger pain and make the sound more crisp.
- Use your middle finger to cover the hole on the back to create a WAH sound.
- Train your thumb to move easily between all the keys on each side.

8-NOTE KALIMBA IN C SCALE

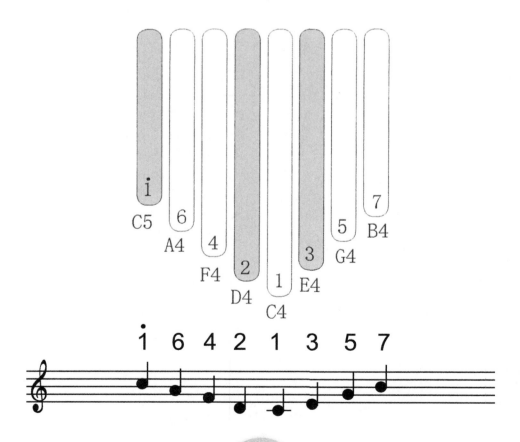

STANDARD 10-NOTE KALIMBA IN C SCALE

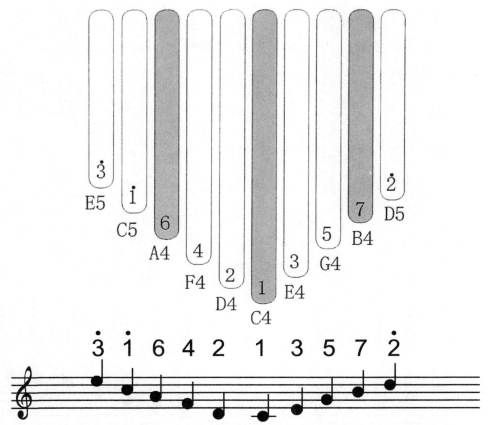

On most 8-10-tine kalimbas, the center tine will be a C note.

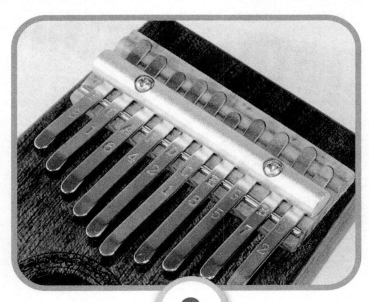

STANDARD 17-NOTE KALIMBA IN C SCALE

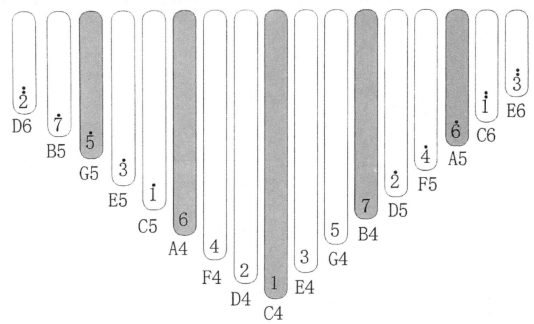

Our sheet music is universal and suitable for 8-17 note kalimbas.

Each of the modern kalimbas usually has engraved numbers and letters representing the name of the notes. The standard 17 note kalimba contains 3 octaves:
1) a full 2nd small octave,
2) a 3rd small octave, and
3) 3 notes from the 4th small octave.

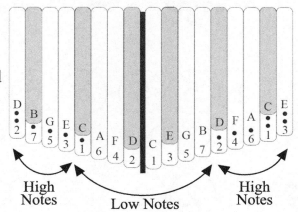

The 2nd small octave goes from C4 to C5 and is depicted in our sheet music as simple numbers. The notes from the 3rd small octave have numbers with one dot above each number. The 3 notes from the 4th small octave - C6, D6, and E6 - are depicted by numbers with two dots above them.

This book includes 65 familiar and easy-to-play songs and melodies. Most songs have been simplified and transposed for one octave. Since this book is aimed at the absolute beginners without any knowledge of reading music, we do not use here the classical music staff and do not show the note durations. You can experiment with a duration on your own.

We call this series "I don't read music" since we are targeting beginners of all ages: children, teens, parents, grandparents.

Folk music traditionally is not learned from sheet music or notes. Instead, it is learned by repetition and from being passed from generation to generation. We believe in this method of teaching, which is easier and more enjoyable. The simple method of using circles as an aid allows the flexibility that existed in traditional ways of teaching.

We recommend finding each of these songs on YouTube and listening to the rhythm before beginning to play. Our sheet music is only a guide. The most important thing is to listen and repeat the recordings.

Alphabet Song

(1) (1) (5) (5) (6) (6) (5) (4) (4) (3) (3)

A - B - C - D   E - F - G   H - I - J - K

(2) (2) (2) (2) (1) (5) (5) (4) (3) (3) (2)

L - M - N - O - P   Q - R - S   T - U - V

(5) (5) (4) (3) (3) (2) (1) (1) (5) (5)

W - X   Y and Z.   Now I know my

(6) (6) (5) (4) (4) (3) (3) (2) (2) (1)

A   B   C's. Next time won't you sing with me.

A Hunting We Will Go

(7) (6) (5) (5) (5) (5)

A   hunting   we   will   go,

(5) (5) (6) (6) (6) (6)

A   hunting   we   will   go.

(6) (6) (7) (7) (7) (7)

We'll catch a fox and put

(i) (i) (i) (i) (i) (i)

him in a box.   And then

(7) (7) (6) (6) (5)

we'll   let him   go.

*The dots above the numbers
mean the notes of another
octave (not the main octave).

A Sailor Went to Sea

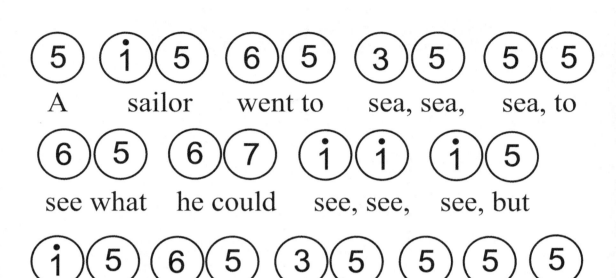

⑤ ⓘ ⑤ ⑥ ⑤ ③ ⑤ ⑤ ⑤
A   sailor   went to   sea, sea,   sea, to

⑥ ⑤ ⑥ ⑦ ⓘ ⓘ ⓘ ⑤
see what   he could   see, see,   see, but

ⓘ ⑤ ⑥ ⑤ ③ ⑤ ⑤ ⑤ ⑤
all that   he could   see, see,   see, was   the

⑥ ⑥ ⑥ ⑥ ⑦ ⑦ ⓘ ⓘ ⓘ
bottom   of   the   deep blue   sea, sea,   sea.

Acka Backa

(5) (5) (6) (6)   (5) (5) (3) (3)

Acka   Backa   soda   cracker

(5) (5) (6) (6)   (5)

Acka   Backa   Boo.

(5) (5) (6) (6)   (5) (5) (3) (3)

Acka   Backa   soda   cracker

(5)   (5)   (3)

Out   goes   you!

Are You Sleeping?

① ② ③ ①   ① ② ③ ①
Are you sleeping,   are you sleeping?

③ ④ ⑤   ③ ④ ⑤
Brother   John,   Brother   John?

⑤ ⑥ ⑤ ④ ③ ①
Morning   bells   are   ringing,

⑤ ⑥ ⑤ ④ ③ ①
Morning   bells   are   ringing

② ⑤ ①   ② ⑤ ①
Ding ding dong,   ding ding dong.

Baa Baa Black Sheep

(1) (1) (5) (5) (6) (6) (6) (6) (5)

Baa, Baa, black sheep, have you any wool?

(4) (4) (3) (3) (2) (2) (1)

Yes sir, yes sir, three bags full.

(5) (5) (5) (4) (4) (3) (3) (3) (2)

One for the master, one for the dame,

(5) (5) (5) (4) (4) (4) (4)

one for the little boy, who

(3) (3) (3) (2)

lives down the lane.

Baby Bumble Bee

(1) (4) (6) (5) (4) (2) (2) (1) (1) (4)

I'm bringing home a   baby   bumble bee

(5) (5) (6) (6) (5) (6) (5) (3) (2)

Won't my mommy be   so proud of me,

(1) (4) (6) (5) (4) (2) (2)

I'm bringing home a   baby

(1) (1) (4)

bumble bee.

Bell Horses

⑤ ③ ③ ⑤ ③ ③

Bell   horses,   bell   horses,

⑤ ⑤ ⑥ ⑥ ⑤

What's the   time of   day?

⑤ ⑤ ③ ⑤ ⑤ ③

One o'clock,   two o'clock,

⑤ ⑤ ⑥ ⑥ ⑤

Time   to go a - way.

Bim Bum Biddy

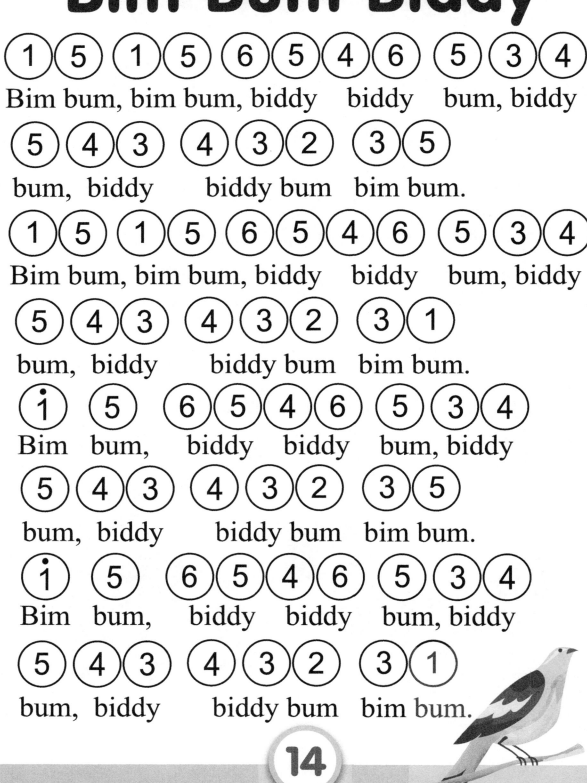

① ⑤ ① ⑤ ⑥ ⑤ ④ ⑥ ⑤ ③ ④
Bim bum, bim bum, biddy biddy bum, biddy

⑤ ④ ③ ④ ③ ② ③ ⑤
bum, biddy biddy bum bim bum.

① ⑤ ① ⑤ ⑥ ⑤ ④ ⑥ ⑤ ③ ④
Bim bum, bim bum, biddy biddy bum, biddy

⑤ ④ ③ ④ ③ ② ③ ①
bum, biddy biddy bum bim bum.

①̇ ⑤ ⑥ ⑤ ④ ⑥ ⑤ ③ ④
Bim bum, biddy biddy bum, biddy

⑤ ④ ③ ④ ③ ② ③ ⑤
bum, biddy biddy bum bim bum.

①̇ ⑤ ⑥ ⑤ ④ ⑥ ⑤ ③ ④
Bim bum, biddy biddy bum, biddy

⑤ ④ ③ ④ ③ ② ③ ①
bum, biddy biddy bum bim bum.

14

Bobby Shafto

⑤ ⑤ ⑥ ⑥ ⑤ ⑤ ③

Bobby   Shafto's gone to sea,

⑤ ⑤ ⑥ ⑥ ⑤ ⑤ ③

Silver   buckles   on his knee.

⑤ ⑤ ⑥ ⑥ ⑤ ⑤ ③

He'll come back and marry me.

⑤ ⑤ ⑥ ⑥ ⑤ ③

Bonnie   Bobby   Shafto!

Brahms' Lullaby

③ ③⑤ ③ ③ ⑤

Lullaby, and good night,

③ ⑤ ①̇ ⑦ ⑥ ⑥ ⑤

With pink roses bedight,

② ③④ ② ② ③④

With lilies o'er spread,

② ④ ⑦ ⑥ ⑤ ⑦ ①̇

Is my baby's sweet head.

① ① ①̇ ⑥ ④ ⑤

Lay you down now, and rest,

③ ① ④ ⑤ ⑥ ⑤

May your slumber be blessed!

① ① ①̇ ⑥ ④ ⑤

Lay you down now, and rest,

③ ① ④ ③ ② ①

May your slumber be blessed!

Chumbara

(1)(1) (1)(3) (2)(1)

Chumbara,   chumbara,

(5)(5)(5)(5) (4)(3)

chumbara,   chumbara

(2)(2)(2)(4)(3)(2)

Chumbara,   chumbara,

(1)(i) (7)(6) (5)(4) (3)(2)

chum, chum, chum, chum, chum, chum

(1)(1) (1)(3) (2)(1)

Chumbara,   chumbara,

(5)(5)(5)(5) (4)(3)

chumbara,   chumbara

(2)(2)(2)(4)(3)(2) (1) (i) (1)

Chumbara, chumbara, chum, chum, chum

Cobbler, Mend My Shoe

(1)(1)(5)(5)(6)(6)(5)(4)(4)(3)(3)

Cobbler, cobbler, mend my shoe. Get it done by

(2)(2)(1)(5)(5)(4)(4)(3)(3)(2)

half past two. Stitch it up and stitch it down

(5)(5)(4)(4)(3)(3)(2)(1)(1)(5)(5)

then I'll give you half a crown. Cobbler, cobbler,

(6)(6)(5)(4)(4)(3)(3)(2)(2)(1)

mend my shoe. Get it done by half past two.

Cock-a-Doodle Doo

(1)(3)(3)(2)(3)(3)(1)(3)(3)(2)(3)

Cock-a-doodle doo, my dame has lost her shoe,

(3)(1̇)(1̇)(7)(6)(5)(3)(1)(2)

and master's lost his fiddling stick and

(3)　(5)(3)(2)(1)(1)　(1)(3)　(3)(2)

doesn't know what to do. And doesn't know what to

(3)(3)　(5)(6)　(5)(3)(5)(5)

do. and doesn't know what to do. The

(1̇)(1̇)(7)(6)(5)(3)(1)(2)

master's lost his fiddling stick and

(3)　(5)(3)(2)(1)

doesn't know what to do.

Cotton Eyed Joe

⑦ ⑦ ⑦ ⑥ ⑤ ⑦ ⑦ ⑦ ②

Where do you come from, where do you go?

⑦ ⑦ ⑦ ⑥ ⑤ ② ③ ⑤ ⑤

Where do you come from, cotton-eyed Joe?

⑦ ⑦ ⑦ ⑥ ⑤ ⑦ ⑦ ⑦ ②

Come for to see you, come for to sing,

⑦ ⑦ ⑦ ⑥ ⑥ ⑤ ② ③ ⑤ ⑤

come for to show you my diamond ring.

Ding Dong DiggiDiggiDong

(1̇) (5) (6)(6)(6)(6) (5)

Ding, dong,　diggidiggi　　dong

(3)(3)(3)(3) (2)(3) (1)(1)　(5)

Diggidiggi　dong, the cat, she's gone!

(1̇) (5) (6)(6)(6)(6) (5)

Ding, dong,　diggidiggi　　dong,

(3)(3)(3)(3) (2)　(3)　(1)

Diggi　diggi　ding, dang dong.

21

Do You Know the Muffin Man?

(1) (1) (4) (4) (5) (6) (4) (4)

Oh, do you know the muf-fin man,

(3) (2) (5) (5) (4) (3) (1) (1)

The muf-fin man, the muf-fin man.

(1) (1) (4) (4) (5) (6) (4) (4)

Oh, do you know the muf-fin man,

(4) (5) (5) (1) (1) (4)

That lives on Dru-ry Lane?

Doggie Doggie

(5) (5) (3) (3) (5) (5) (3)

Doggie,   doggie, where's your bone?

(5) (5) (5) (3) (6) (5) (5) (3)

Somebody   stole   it   from your home.

(5) (3) (6) (5) (3)

Who has my   bone?

(5) (3) (6) (5) (3)

I   have your   bone.

Dr. Foster

(5) (3) (5) (3) (5) (6) (5) (3)

Doctor Foster went to Gloucester

(5) (5) (6) (6) (6) (5) (3)

in a shower of rain,

(1) (1) (1) (1) (1) (1)

Stepped in a puddle right

(6) (6) (6) (5) (5) (5) (5)

up to his middle and he

(5) (5) (5) (3) (2) (1)

never went there again.

Fiddle-Dee-Dee

(3)(1)(1) (1)(3)(1) (1) (1)(1)

Fiddle dee dee, Fiddle dee dee, The

(2)(2)(5) (5)(5)(3)(1) (1)(1)(1)

fly has married the bumble bee. Said the

(6)(6)(6) (6)(6) (6)(5) (5)(5)

fly, said he, "Will you marry me? And

(5)(4)(4) (5)(4)(3)(3) (3)(1)(1)(1)

live with me, sweet bumble bee?"Fiddle dee dee,

(3)(1)(1) (1)(1)(2)(2) (5)(5)(5)

Fiddle dee dee, the fly has married the

(3)(1)(1)

bumble bee.

Five Little Ducks

③ ② ② ① ① ⑦ ⑥ ⑤

Five little ducks went out one day,

⑤ ① ① ④ ③ ③ ② ②

Over   the hill and far away

③ ③ ② ① ① ⑦ ⑥ ⑤ ⑤

Mother duck said, "Quack, quack, quack, quack", and

⑤ ① ④ ③ ③ ② ② ①

only   four   little   ducks came back.

Five Little Monkeys

① ⑥ ⑥ ⑤ ⑥ ① ① ⑥ ⑥ ⑤

Five little monkeys jumping on the bed,

① ⑥ ⑤ ⑥ ③ ② ① ①

one fell off and bumped his head. So

① ① ⑥ ⑥ ⑤ ⑤ ⑥ ⑥ ① ⑥ ⑤

mommy called the doctor and the doctor said,

① ⑥ ⑤ ⑥ ③ ③ ② ② ①

"No more monkey jumping one the bed!"

27

Frog in the Meadow

(7) (7) (7) (6) (5)

Frog in the meadow,

(7) (7) (7) (5)

can't get him out.

(7) (7) (7) (7) (6) (5)

Take a little stick and

(7) (7) (7) (5)

stir him about.

Good Night, Ladies

⑦ ⑤ ② ⑤ ⑦ ⑤ ⑥ ⑥

Good night, ladies! Good night, ladies!

⑦ ⑤ ①̇ ①̇ ①̇ ⑦ ⑦ ⑦ ⑥ ⑥ ⑤

Good night, ladies, we're going to   leave you now.

⑦ ⑥ ⑤   ⑥   ⑦   ⑦ ⑦

   Merrily   we   roll   along,

⑥ ⑥ ⑥ ⑦ ②̇ ②̇ ⑦ ⑥ ⑤ ⑥

roll   along,   roll   along,   merrily   we

⑦ ⑦ ⑦   ⑥ ⑥ ⑦ ⑥   ⑤

roll   along,   o'er the dark blue   sea.

Happy Birthday

①①②　①④③
Happy　　birthday　to　you,

①①②　①⑤④
Happy　　birthday　to　you,

①①î　⑥④④③②
Happy　　birthday　　dear　　Mary,

îî⑥　④⑤④
Happy　　birthday　to　you!

30

Hot Cross Buns

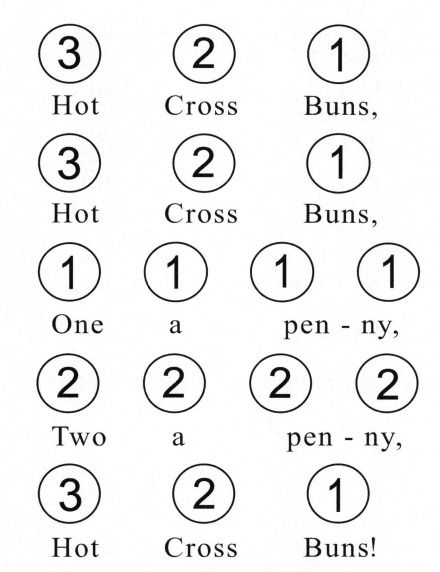

③ ② ①
Hot Cross Buns,

③ ② ①
Hot Cross Buns,

① ① ① ①
One a pen - ny,

② ② ② ②
Two a pen - ny,

③ ② ①
Hot Cross Buns!

Humpty Dumpty

(1)(1) (3)(3) (2)(3)(2) (1)

Humpty Dumpty sat on a wall,

(3)(3) (5)(5) (4)(5)(4) (3)

Humpty Dumpty had a great fall;

(6)(6)(6) (5)(5)(5) (4)(4)(4) (3)

All the king's horses and all the king's men

(2)(3)(4) (5)(3)(1) (2)(3)(2) (1)

Couldn't put Humpty together again.

I Like to Eat Apples and Bananas

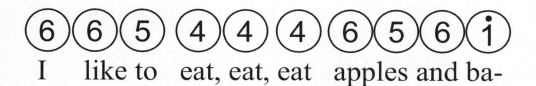

⑥ ⑥ ⑤ ④ ④ ④ ⑥ ⑤ ⑥ ①

I   like to   eat, eat, eat   apples and ba-

⑥ ⑤   ⑤ ⑤ ④ ③ ③ ③

nanas,   I   like to eat, eat, eat

⑤ ④ ⑤ ⑥   ⑤ ④   ⑥ ⑥ ⑤

apples and ba - nanas   I   like to

I Love Little Kitty

③ ④ ⑤ ⑤ ⑤ ⑤ i̇ ⑦ ⑥ ② ②
I   love little   kitty, Her coat is so

② ③ ④ ④ ④ ④ ⑦ ⑥
warm, And   if   I don't hurt her, She'll

⑤ ③ ③ ③ ③ ④ ⑤ ⑤ ⑤
do me no   harm. So I'll   not pull her

⑤ i̇ ⑦ ⑥ ② ② ② ③
tail,   Nor   drive her a-way, But

④ ⑦ ⑥ ⑤ ③ ② ① i̇ i̇
kitty and   I,   very   gently will play.

It's Raining

⑤ ⑤ ③ ⑥ ⑤ ③ ③

It's raining, it's pouring, the

⑤ ③ ⑥ ⑤ ③

old man is snoring.

⑤ ⑤ ③ ③ ⑥ ⑤ ⑤ ③ ③ ⑥

Went to bed and he bumped his head and he

⑤ ⑤ ⑤ ③ ③ ⑥ ⑤ ③

couldn't get up in the morning.

Itsy Bitsy Spider

① ① ① ① ② ③ ③

The itsy - bitsy spider

③ ② ① ② ③ ①

Climbed up the water spout.

③ ③ ④ ⑤

Down came the rain

⑤ ④ ③ ④ ⑤ ③

And washed the spider out.

① ① ② ③

Out came the sun

③ ② ① ② ③ ①

And dried up all the rain

① ① ① ① ② ③ ③

And the itsy - bitsy spider

③ ② ① ② ③ ①

Climbed up the spout again.

Jack and Jill

① ① ② ② ③ ③ ④ ④
Jack and Jill went up the hill, to

⑤ ⑤ ⑥ ⑥ ⑦ ⓘ
fetch a pail of water

ⓘ ⓘ ⑦ ⑦ ⑥ ⑥ ⑤ ⑤
Jack fell down and broke his crown and

④ ④ ③ ③ ② ①
Jill came tumbling after.

Jingle Bells

(3) (3) (3)   (3) (3) (3)

Jingle   bells,   jingle bells,

(3) (5) (1) (2) (3)

Jingle   all the way.

(4) (4) (4) (4) (4) (3) (3)

Oh, what fun it   is to ride

(3) (3) (2) (2) (3) (2) (5)

In   a   one horse open   sleigh.

(3) (3) (3)   (3) (3) (3)

Jingle   bells,   jingle   bells,

(3) (5) (1) (2) (3)

Jingle   all the way.

(4) (4) (4) (4) (4) (3) (3)

Oh, what fun it is to ride

(3) (5) (5) (4) (2) (1)

In a one horse   open   sleigh.

Jolly Old Saint Nicholas

(6) (6) (6) (6)   (5) (5) (5)
Jolly   old Saint   Nicholas

(4)   (4)   (4)   (4)   (6)
Lean   your   ear   this   way.

(2)   (2)   (2)   (2)   (1)   (1)   (4)
Don't   you   tell   a   single   soul

(5)   (4)   (5)   (6)   (5)
What   I'm going   to say.

(6)   (6)   (6)   (6)   (5)   (5)   (5)
Christmas   Eve   is   coming   soon.

(4)   (4)   (4)   (4)   (6)
Now,   you   dear   old   man,

(2)   (2)   (2)   (2)   (1)   (1) (4)
Whisper   what   you'll   bring   to   me.

(5)   (4)   (5)   (6)   (4)
Tell   me   if   you   can.

MERRY CHRISTMAS

Kookaburra

(5) (5) (5) (5) (6)
Kookaburra   sits

(6) (6) (5) (3) (5) (3)
on   the   old   gum   tree.

(3) (3) (3) (3) (4)
Merry   merry   King

(4) (4) (3) (1) (3) (1)
of   the   bush   is   he.

(i) (6) (7) (i) (6)
Laugh,   Kookaburra,

(5)   (5) (6) (5) (4)
Laugh,   Kookaburra,

(3) (1) (1) (1) (1)
Happy your   life   must   be.

40

La Cucaracha

(1) (1) (1) (4) (6) (1) (1) (1) (4) (6)

La   cu - ca - ra - cha,   la   cu - ca - ra - cha

(4)   (4) (3) (3) (2) (2) (1)

Ya   no   puede   caminar,

(1) (1) (1) (3) (5) (1) (1) (1) (3) (5)

Porque   no   tiene,   porque   le   falta

(i)   (i) (i) (i) (6) (5) (4)

Dos   patitos   para   andar.

41

Little Jack Horner

①①①④③②②②⑤④

Little Jack Horner sat in the corner,

③③③ ⑥⑤④ ①

Eating a Christmas pie; He

①①①④ ③②②②⑤ ④

put in his thumb, and pulled out a plum, And

③③③ ③②③ ④

said, "What a good boy am I!"

London Bridge Is Falling Down

(5) (6) (5) (4) (3) (4) (5)

London   Bridge   is   falling   down,

(2) (3) (4) (3) (4) (5)

Falling   down,   falling   down.

(5) (6) (5) (4) (3) (4) (5)

London   Bridge   is   falling   down,

(2) (5) (3) (1)

My   fair   lady.

43

Mary Had a Little Lamb

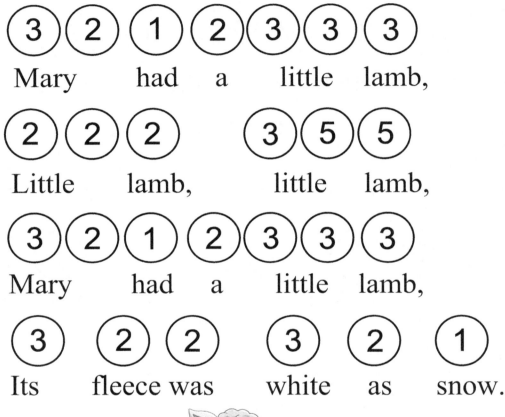

(3) (2) (1) (2) (3) (3) (3)
Mary   had   a   little   lamb,

(2) (2) (2)   (3) (5) (5)
Little   lamb,   little   lamb,

(3) (2) (1) (2) (3) (3) (3)
Mary   had   a   little   lamb,

(3) (2) (2) (3) (2) (1)
Its   fleece was   white   as   snow.

Miss Mary Mack

(5) (6) (7) (i) (i) (i)

Miss   Mary   Mack, Mack, Mack,

(5) (6) (7) (i) (i) (i)

all   dressed in   black, black, black,

(5) (6) (7) (i) (i) (i) (i) (i) (i)

with   silver   buttons,   buttons,   buttons

(5) (6) (7) (i) (i) (i)

all   down   her   back, back, back!

45

My Hat

⑤ ⑥ ⑤ ④ ③ ④ ② ③
My hat it has three corners; Three

④⑤ ⑥⑤ ③ ⑤ ①⑤ ④③
corners has my hat, And had it not three

④② ③ ④⑤⑥⑤ ①
corners, it would not be my hat.

46

Ninety-Nine Bottles

(4)(4)(4) (1)(1)(1) (4)(4)(4) (4)

Ninety-nine   bottles of   pop   on   the   wall,

(5)(5)(5) (2)(2)(2) (5)

Ninety-nine   bottles of   pop.

(3) (3) (3) (3)(3)(3) (3)

Take one down,   pass it   around,

(1)(1)(1) (2)(2)(3) (4)(4)(4)(4)

Ninety-eight   bottles of   pop on   the   wall.

No more bottles of pop on the wall,
no more bottles of pop.
Go to the store and buy some more,
99 bottles of pop on the wall...

Ode to Joy

(3) (3) (4) (5) (5) (4) (3) (2)

(1) (1) (2) (3) (3)   (2)(2)

(3) (3) (4) (5) (5) (4) (3) (2)

(1) (1) (2) (3) (2)   (1)(1)

(2) (2) (3) (1) (2) (3)(4)(3) (1)

(2)   (3)(4)(3)   (2) (1) (2) (5)

(3) (3) (4) (5) (5) (4) (3) (2)

(1) (1) (2) (3) (2)   (1)(1)

48

Oh! Susannah

① ② ③ ⑤ ⑤⑥⑤③

Well! I come from   A-la-ba-ma

① ② ③③ ② ① ②

With my ban-jo on my knee,

①②③⑤⑤⑥⑤③

I'm going   to Louis-i-a-na

①②③③②②①

My true love   for to see.

④ ④ ⑥ ⑥

Oh!   Su-san-nah,

⑤   ⑤ ③①②

Don't you cry for me

①②③⑤⑤⑥⑤③

I   come from A-la-ba-ma

① ②③③②②①

With my ban-jo on my knee.

49

Oh We Can Play on the Big Bass Drum

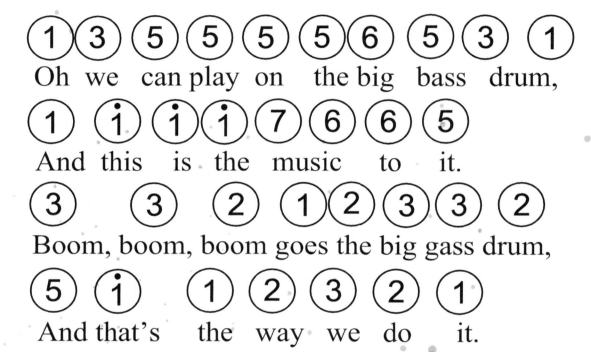

(1) (3) (5) (5) (5) (5) (6) (5) (3) (1)
Oh we can play on the big bass drum,

(1) (i̇) (i̇) (i̇) (7) (6) (6) (5)
And this is the music to it.

(3) (3) (2) (1) (2) (3) (3) (2)
Boom, boom, boom goes the big gass drum,

(5) (i̇) (1) (2) (3) (2) (1)
And that's the way we do it.

50

Old Bald Eagle

(4) (4) (4) (4) (4) (4) (1)

Old bald eagle sail around,

(4) (3) (4) (5)

daylight is gone.

(3) (3) (3) (3) (3) (3) (1)

Old bald eagle sail around,

(6) (6) (5) (4)

daylight is gone.

Two bald eagles...

Three bald eagles...

Four bald eagles...

Old Blue

③ ③ ③ ③ ① ① ③ ③ ⑤

I had a dog and his name was Blue,

③ ③ ③ ③ ① ① ② ② ①

I had a dog and his name was Blue.

③ ③ ③ ③ ① ① ③ ③ ⑤ ⑤ ⑤

I had a dog and his name was Blue, And I

③ ③ ③ ③ ③ ① ① ② ② ①

betcha five dollars he's a good dog too.

⑤ ③ ① ② ② ①

Here Blue! You good dog you.

Old MacDonald Had a Farm

(5) (5) (5) (2) (3) (3) (2)
Old McDonald   had a farm.

(7)(7)(6)(6)(5)
E - I - E - I - O

(2) (5) (5) (5) (2) (3)(3)(2)
And on   that farm he had a cow.

(7)(7)(6)(6)(5)
E - I - E - I - O

(2) (2) (5) (5) (5)
With a moo moo here.

(2) (2) (5) (5) (5)
With a moo moo there.

(5)(5)(5)
Here a moo.

(5)(5)(5)
There a moo.

(5)(5)(5)(5)(5) (5)
Everywhere a moo moo.

(5)(5)(5)(2)(3)(3)(2)
Old McDonald   had a farm.

What does a cow say?
Meow?
Oink?
Moo?

(7)(7)(6)(6)(5)
E - I - E - I - O

Old Mother Hubbard

(4)(4)(4) (4)(3) (4) (5)(5)(5)

Old Mother Hubbard, She went to the

(5)(4)(5) (6)(6)(6) (i)(7)(6)(5) (1)

cupboard to get her poor dog a bone. But

(4) (4) (4) (4) (4) (5)(5) (5)(5) (5)

when she got there the cupboard was bare, And

(6)(5)(4) (3)(4)(5) (4)

so the poor dog had none.

One, Two, Three, Four

⑥ ⑥ ⑤ ④ ④
One, two, three, four, five

① ④ ⑥ ⑥ ⑥ ⑥ ⑦
once I caught a fish alive.

⑥ ⑦ ⑦ ⑥ ⑤ ⑤
Six, seven, eight, nine, ten,

④ ③ ② ③ ⑤ ④ ④
then I let it go again.

Rain, Rain, Go Away

(5) (3)   (5) (5) (3)

Rain, rain,   go   away,

(5) (5) (3) (6) (5) (5) (3)

Come again   a - nother   day,

(4) (4) (2) (2) (4) (4) (2)

Little   children wants to play,

(5) (4) (3) (2) (3) (1) (1)

Rain,   rain   go   away.

Ring Around the Rosie

(5)(5)(3)(6)(5)(3)(3)

Ring around the rosie, A

(5)(5)(3)(6)(5)(3)

pocket full of posies,

(5)(3)(5)(3)(3)

Atishoo! Atishoo! We

(5)(5)(1)

all fall down!

Row, Row, Row Your Boat

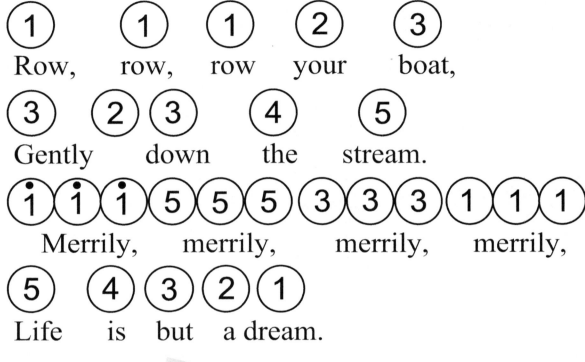

① ① ① ② ③
Row,   row,   row   your   boat,

③ ② ③ ④ ⑤
Gently   down   the   stream.

①① ①① ①① ⑤ ⑤ ⑤ ③ ③ ③ ① ① ①
Merrily,   merrily,   merrily,   merrily,

⑤ ④ ③ ② ①
Life   is   but   a dream.

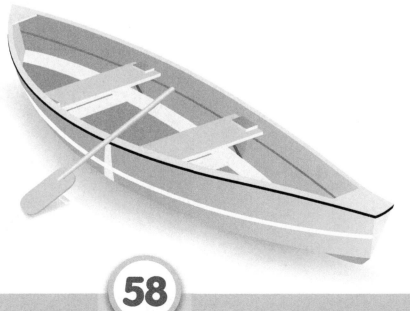

Rub-a-Dub-Dub

①①① ① ① ③③③③

Rub-a-dub - dub,   three men in   a   tub,

③ ⑤⑤⑤ ⑤ ⑤ ⑤ ⑤

And   who do you   think   they   be?

⑤ ①①① ⑤⑤⑤

The   butcher, the   baker, the

③③③ ①①①

candlestick   maker, and

⑤⑤④ ③ ② ①

all   of them   gone   to   sea.

See-Saw Margery Daw

(5) (3) (5) (5) (5) (3)

See-saw, Margery Daw

(5) (5) (3) (3) (6) (5) (3)

Jack shall have a new master.

(5) (5) (3) (3) (3) (5) (5) (5) (3) (3)

He shall have but a penny a day, Be-

(5) (5) (5) (3) (3) (6) (5) (3)

cause he won't work any faster.

Ten in the Bed

(1) (1) (4) (4) (4) (4) (1) (1)

There were ten in the bed and the

(4) (4) (4) (4) (i) (6) (4)

little   one said, "Roll   over,

(i) (6) (4) (1) (1) (4) (4)

"Roll over,   So they all rolled

(4) (4) (1) (4) (4) (4)

over   and one fell out.

The Bee and the Pup

⑤ ⑤ ③ ① ① ① ① ① ⑤ ⑤ ③

There was   a   bee - i - ee - i - ee Sat on   a

② ② ② ② ② ⑤ ⑥ ⑤

wall-i - all - i - all And he went

⑦ ⑦ ⑦ ⑦ ⑦ ⑤ ⑥ ⑦

buzz-i - uzz - i -uzz   And that was

①̇ ①̇ ①̇ ①̇ ①̇

all - i - all - i - all!

The Big Sheep

(5) (7) (6) (5) (3) (2) (2) (2) (3) (5)

As I went to market on one market

(6) (5) (7) (7) (6) (5) (3) (2) (2)

day, I saw as big a sheep, sir as

(2) (2) (3) (4) (5) (5) (7) (5) (6) (5)

ever fed on hay. Oh, farearaddy

(3) (2) (2) (2) (2) (3) (5) (6) (5)

daddy, Oh farearaddy hay. Oh,

(7) (5) (6) (5) (3) (2) (2)

farearaddy daddy, Oh

(2) (2) (3) (5) (5)

farearaddy day.

63

The Mulberry Bush

(4)(4)(4) (4) (6) (1)(1)(6) (4)

Here we go round the mulberry bush,

(4) (5)(5)(5) (5) (6) (5)(5)(3) (1)

the mulberry bush, the mulberry bush,

(4)(4)(4) (4) (6) (1)(1)(6) (4)

Here we go round the mulberry bush,

(4) (5)(5) (1)(2)(3) (4) (4)

so early in the morning.

The Wheels on the Bus

(1) (4) (4) (4) (4) (6) (i) (6) (4)

The wheels on   the bus   go round and round.

(5) (3) (1)   (i) (6) (4)

Round and round.   Round and round.

(1) (4) (4) (4) (4) (6) (i) (6) (4)

The wheels on   the   bus   go round and round.

(5) (1) (1) (4)

Round and round.

This Old Man

⑤ ③ ⑤ ⑤ ③ ⑤ ⑥ ⑤ ④ ③

This old man, he played one, He played knick-knack

② ③ ④ ③ ④ ⑤ ① ① ① ①

on my thumb; With a knick-knack paddy whack,

① ② ③ ④ ⑤ ⑤ ② ② ④

Give the dog a bone! This old man came

③ ② ①

rolling home.

Tinga Layo

③ ⑤ ⑥ ⑤ ④ ④ ④ ⑤ ④ ③

Tinga　Layo,　come, little　donkey, come,

③ ⑤ ⑥ ⑤ ② ② ② ③ ② ①

Tinga　Layo,　come, little donkey, come,

⑤ ①̇ ⑦ ⑥ ④ ⑦ ⑥ ⑤

My　donkey　walk, my　donkey talk,

③ ⑥ ⑤ ④ ③ ② ⑤ ④ ③

My　donkey　cut with　a　knife and fork.

③ ⑤ ⑥ ⑤ ④ ④ ④ ⑤ ④ ③

Tinga　Layo, come, little　donkey, come,

③ ⑤ ⑥ ⑤ ② ② ② ③ ② ①

Tinga　Layo,　come, little donkey, come,

⑤ ①̇ ⑦ ② ② ② ③ ② ①

My　donkey,　come, little　donkey, come.

67

To Market, To Market

(5) $(\dot{1})$ (5) (5) $(\dot{1})$ (5) (5) (3) (2) (1) (5)

To market, to market to buy a fat pig.

(6) (7) $(\dot{1})$ (5) (4) (3) (3) (2) (1) (2) (5)

Home again, home again jiggety jig. To

$(\dot{1})$ (5) (5) $(\dot{1})$ (5) (5) (3) (2) (1) (6)

market, to market to buy a fat hog.

(5) (6) (7) $(\dot{1})$ (5) (3) (4) (3) (2) (1)

Home again, home again jiggety jog.

68

Twinkle, Twinkle Little Star

(1) (1) (5) (5) (6) (6) (5)

Twin - kle,   twin - kle   lit - tle   star,

(4) (4) (3) (3) (2) (2) (1)

How   I   won - der   what   you   are.

(5) (5) (4) (4) (3) (3) (2)

Up   a - bove   the   world   so high,

(5) (5) (4) (4) (3) (3) (2)

Like   a   dia - mond   in   the   sky.

We Wish You a Merry Christmas

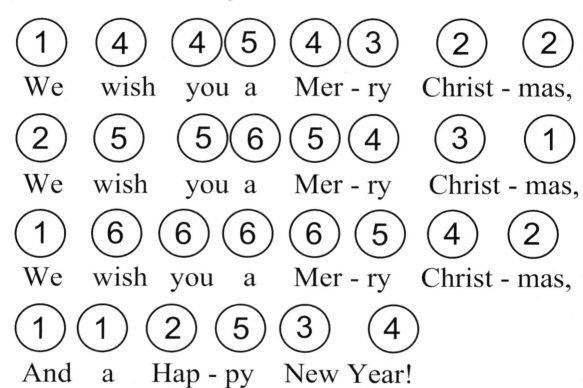

①	④	④	⑤	④	③	②	②
We	wish	you	a	Mer -	ry	Christ -	mas,

②	⑤	⑤	⑥	⑤	④	③	①
We	wish	you	a	Mer -	ry	Christ -	mas,

①	⑥	⑥	⑥	⑥	⑤	④	②
We	wish	you	a	Mer -	ry	Christ -	mas,

①	①	②	⑤	③	④
And	a	Hap -	py	New	Year!

Printed in Great Britain
by Amazon

35580718R00040